Dialogues

THE COURAGE AND WISDOM
TO ASK AND HEAR

TONY BERNARDI

Published by HAP21

Healing Arts for Peace in the 21st Century

www.hap21.com

ISBN: 0983250006
ISBN-13: 9780983250005
LCCN: 2010943518

To

Julian Andres Lasprilla Burbano

Preface

This is an ode to longing. We long for what is sometimes briefly obscured, not unlike the sun that hides behind the clouds of grief for a little while. We long for love or rather for that which welcomes our love. Like the plain canvas beneath a masterpiece, without which the artist cannot create the art, we realize its importance only in the absence of our art making. We are the artists, the lovers. Our work is our love. And our beloved, our canvas. Without them neither our art nor a meaningful life is possible. Perhaps this is why we long.

It is through such longing that we often encounter unknown depths in our inner landscape. One such revelation, chronicled here as a series of fantastic dialogues, was a result of a longing that led me into my darkest night. Blinded by despair I awakened to a new light of honesty, a wisdom within me I had not yet met.

In hindsight, it was simple. I asked and I was answered. And so I understood that my darkness of despair was nothing but a longing for love. This understanding I diligently recorded here in hopes to also aid others. Hence, I offer these dialogues to everyone who bravely dares to reach for the light in the midst of their darkest night, for I know in this daring their understanding will also come. These dialogues illumined the longing I often misconstrued. Having returned from what seems to have been a journey without a distance I happily report what I was looking for, that which I truly am, I found. This, the reason we long, is an inextinguishable love.

Contents

Dialogues   xiii

I.   The next day   1
A dialogue with my True Self

II.   And so generously days follow   7
A dialogue with the Reader

III.   Also the night falls   13
A dialogue with Solitude

IV.   O, you terrifying mirror   19
A conversation with the Mirror

V.   Quietly I asked and was quietly answered   25
A dialogue with God

VI.   Just before the dawn   33
A dialogue with the Devil

VII.   A new day   41
A dialogue with Spring

VIII.   Upon the undeliverable promise   47
A dialogue with Lust

IX.   Come upon my arms to rest   53
A dialogue with Death

X.   Upon a full day's work   59
        A dialogue with the Body

XI.   Upon the sweat of the brow   65
        A dialogue with Work

XII.   Upon the breaking of the bread   73
        A dialogue with Food

XIII.   Upon gentle hands   79
        A dialogue with Love

XIV.   Upon a burdened heart   85
        A dialogue with Grief

XV.   Lost in the joy of our visit   91
        A dialogue with Friendship

XVI.   Broken at your doorsteps   97
        A dialogue with Surrender

XVII.   Upon the brow of the prophet   103
        A dialogue with Faith

XVIII. On the light wings of joy   109
        And a dialogue with Hope

Epilogue   115

Acknowledgments   119

Dialogues

Prologue

It is a cold and wintry January morning around 9:15 am. It has been snowing, and now freezing rain and drizzle keep the vision of winter set in the view from every window of the house. Winter seems as beautiful, calm, and quiet as most of my frozen dreams, which await their awakening.

I set forth to engage in and record a series of dialogues today. I often feel the presence of others around me, but I am not sure who they are. At times I notice my father sitting on the sofa in the living room, or my mother watching over my shoulder as I sit at my desk.

These spirits and perhaps others often move in and out of my room unnoticed. Their purpose I cannot comprehend. Often my nagging needs take me away from noticing anything of significance. These needs of my body and needs of an ever hungry mind can never be fulfilled. This mind I now engage in dialogue, suspecting that is where all my dreams lay frozen in slumber, as I dream of my windows' view in icy silence.

I am determined to create a door out of my prison cell, a cloud out of my rain, and a ladder out of my sorrow. All this is an effort to reach the other side of happiness. This trap of happiness, an unfulfilled and un-fulfill-able promise, keeps me in dreams and my reality in bondage. On the other side, I know I will find joy. Joy is the only meaningful movement, the only dance that matters. I no longer wish to dream of dancing. I am the dance. Happiness is a dream. Joy is the real thing.

Now, I diligently engage in dialogue with living spirits, present or not. What is this dreamy illusion? Why the attraction to this potent poison I call living? I am Life! What business is this illusion of living? How meaningless! Could an apple pretend to be an apple?

I seek to lose my pretense now!

⁕

The next day

A DIALOGUE WITH MY TRUE SELF

❦

The day is still sweet, all but a few minutes short of 3 o'clock in the afternoon. Sunny, but still shy of a warm day. The snow and ice seem to be giggling as they rejoin the waters underground that await them patiently. But still spring is nowhere to be found as both I and the groundhog wait for the predictions only a few days away.

Winter is a kind time of the year. It is kind to rest, to sleep, to practice patience, and most of all, it is good to experience the coming of the light and remain grateful. Perhaps all this is a sign of age, a sign of a maturing heart that is learning to love patiently.

Thinking of all whom I can call forward for my brave dialogue, one name comes to mind over and over as my deep suspicions become more and more a reality. Who is writing all this? And yet there is no one, at least there seems to be no one here in the room with me. My dear companion, I am grateful for your ever present presence that you bestow so graciously upon me.

So this sunny winter day, I know, "He who sent me will direct me" as He is guiding and loving me now. He is always here and now with me. Only when I seem to stray from here and now, my vision, my awareness of Him becomes obscured.

We do not know. It is not only that we have forgotten, but truly I say, "I do not know". There is always newness here. True newness. There appears and disappears what has never been here before. There is a show going on and the view exists, or it is so possible from where I am, here, now. I close my eyes, but even then the sun peeks through the clouds. My wintry day glitters with the sun bravely kissing me and every icy notion that ecstatically awaits resurrection into laughter and dance.

I have to admit, I am a bit scared to start this conversation. I am not sure what I will hear. What or how it will come about. But if I could be brave, only on such sunny days it would be possible.

Yes, I am calling upon my guiding light, the crown of all my knowing. The knowing that goes with me wherever I go. Nothing is hidden from Him, nothing is withheld and nothing is ever judged. However, I still need reassurances. How sweet is His love for me as he reassures me patiently, strongly, yet all but gently, that I am the light of the world.

The light comes when the clouds seem to have melted away, and the burden of remembrance has turned into the joy of knowing. Remember me. I am the flowers that you have always grown. Look at me. Do not take me for granted for what you steal, you steal from your awareness.

My dream of the barren desert has not touched the garden where I gently rest on His chest, comforted by the strength of an inextinguishable love.

❧

And so generously days follow

A DIALOGUE WITH THE READER

Calm wicked heart, calm. So much wanting calls in the clouds, and there are too many clouds in the winter. The sun peeks with a friendly smile reminding me of all the goodness still to come, like packages from heaven.

Yes, today I will to have a dialogue with you the reader. What is it you are looking to find? And although you seem so silent, I know your thoughts and your mind are a raging ocean. Calm as it seems, the undercurrents are strong and call you to a thousand directions all at once. How do I know that, you ask? Strange as it seems, we share the same ocean. Your call is my call, and although I insist that I travel alone, your persistent presence is the ocean that enables my travels. And although I often neglect to admit, the reason and destination of all my movements is you my dear reader. How more intimate can we get?

The sun rises from the east and sets to the west, and all seems to be so predictable. But I ask you, what is so predictable? Of course I am really asking this from both of us. What is so predictable about you and me? I am willing to share with you, the most precious, most tender intimate parts of what I believe to be me. And you just observe, read. But we cannot connect because time has cut us apart like a knife that severs the limbs of a corpse.

I am alone only because you have not yet read anything I have to say. But as you read this I become part of you in a way that I could not in another, even if you let me have your most precious possession. Now we have both become the reader, for how can I ignore you when all I can do is to tell you our story.

Now I have to let you speak. What would you say? Enough is enough? How do I dare to make such assumptions? Gross preconceptions and all in ignorance? Could it be that our intimacy has brought about an awareness in me enabling me to know you even better than myself?

Joy is what I seek and not you, I tell you in earnest.
When I think of you my joy disappears. All I can
see and feel is my fragmented self. The part of me
that is writing this, and you who are reading this
now. And now, our now has become now. Now we
are one and yes now, somehow I feel healed again.
By your reading this we become one and I lose my
sense of fragmentation. We become one.

I am tempted to tell you about my story, our story,
but all I have to report is the weather. The sun is
shining. Life is smiling. The clouds are dancing
in the frigid air of a wintry morning sliding softly
into noon. I wonder where you are now. Are you
sitting softly on a comfortable chair, reading me as I
am writing for you? Are you well? I wish you could
understand how much I miss you, but I guess you do
because you are still reading.

I have to admit that indeed all is well. Our separation is not permanent. By all expert accounts we
will be reunited soon. Perhaps we are breaking the
time and space barriers as I am writing these words

and as you are reading them. I thank you for returning my most precious part of myself to me. I feel complete now. No letter is complete until it is read. And completely and thoroughly read. Keep reading, dear kind reader, for that is the only way we can join and become one. I am grateful you have arrived.

Also the night falls

A DIALOGUE WITH SOLITUDE

cy/o

Tell me dark room, why have you been so carelessly abandoned by the light? Where has the day gone and how long do you have to wait for what is rightfully yours? Is darkness your primary occupation?

I am the comforter of lies and the hiding place of liars. Here only one thing matters and that is the not knowing. No one has a choice in me other than to sleep in the comfort of the everlasting trust. Calm emptiness is what I pretend to offer and, indeed, when one looks in the dark, only then emptiness becomes obvious.

This emptiness is lost in the busyness of the playful light. Here there is comfort and rest and loneliness. I am the only one keeping a watchful eye on all who come and stay. It takes courage to remain in me, it takes trust. Who can trust more than the ones hiding from the light?

All the drawn curtains tell how the liars' secrets are safe. In darkness everyone is the same. In the emptiness of my dark space I contain everything within me without the burden of judgment, without the sound of the scales measuring every thing and everyone in the revealing light.

You see, sight is no gift to people who totally trust, and in the dark room one has to totally trust. How about fear, you ask? Fear of the unknown? Where nothing is known, there is no conflict. There is no degree of madness. There is the emptiness. What can one do but to surrender to the darkness? When the light falls away from the eyes, you enter me. I am the dark room. Never fear the dark room, but beware of the dark mind.

A dark mind is not empty, but full of all that is not light. A dark room has no shades of light. A dark mind is not dark with emptiness, but dim with shades of darkness and half light. No one can rest in a dark mind. That is where the liar sets his workshop and builds the base of his destruction.

Do not be wary of the dark room. I am dark to the eyes so you can light me with the vision of your heart, and then you will see me as how I really am, luminous. Just like the empty canvas unsoiled by deceptive color, I become the bride of your Christ light.

You are welcome, liar or not! I give you comfort, solace, shelter, and I purify your eyes where the cobweb of greed has gathered for eons. Here you can not see anything that is not in your heart. Here you have to trust me for I know that hidden behind your false light shines your light of truth. Only in the dark room, in the comfort of our solitude we become accustomed to our eternal purple flame and meet each other in earnest, naked. And so we experience each other as intimately as we know the breath of our creator.

In the dark room we can both remember and forget. There is little choice when all light is lost and no lie can be revealed. I tell you, all your lies are irrelevant, forgotten, wiped clean in my darkness. And so what remains in you is your naked pure perfection.

The dark room is your friend. Do not shy away. Enter often and be cleansed. I know all the lies before you thought of them. I know them so that you will never have to. Come and rest awhile. There is more room. Come. Come now.

O, you terrifying mirror

A CONVERSATION WITH THE MIRROR

Almost midday and off I go looking for a face to put on. Now, who was I yesterday? Let me remember. And today, late into the day, I dare to look and find "I", that illusive eye that mirrors back what the real mirror tries to hide.

My faithful looking glass, what I look to see is taken away by all the flattery I refused and all the lies I am ready to accept today. O, you terrifying mirror, tell me what have you to say on all this? Be gentle, but say. Please dare to say.

Look closely in my heart. Do you see the light reflected there, where you do not want to see? That wrinkle, that hair? Yes you are that deformed, crumbled being forgotten through the night, when you set out to search for your illusive dreamy self. What happened? Did you find what you were looking for? Where is that fleeing perfection today? Why did you trade the night for the day? Now you see all that you can see in me, and the perfect face, that dream, is no longer there. Who are you then? Are you your kind friend you refused that day? Are you the enemy you feared yesterday? What don't you like? Tell me, and I can show you something else.

In me everything is possible. My job is to reflect. But make you not a mistake: I only reflect your ideas, for you are blind to everything else. Do you see?

Hell I raise, all your fear, and angels scatter away? Alas, the mirror is never empty and yet it holds nothing. That is why it can do well what it is meant to do. And that is to reflect what can for a little while linger, and then change and run away.

Why do you fear and despise me then? Is it my honesty or the lies I say?

Friend, I am your friend today, and everyday. Have you noticed that when you look in me all you see is what you

choose to be that day? **Fear strikes your heart when you
realize there is nothing in me that you do not assume to
be in you, and yet when you look, all you see is a moment fleeing away.** *Look again and you can see a different world reflected there.* **Who is showing you all this? Is
it me or you?** *Or maybe it is you who insists on showing
me my face?* **We look at each other and what we see is a
broken image, tired of all illusions.**

*Pretty face, reflected in my eyes, blinded by grace, an an-
gel standing by me beckoning, asking to reconsider my
gaze.* **Look at me instead, but only if you choose not to
look straight.** *Look at me and not what you consider to
be your face.* **Look at me and see.** *See grace.* **I always
stand beside you, age in and age out.** *Day in and day
out.* **And when you seemingly have died, others would
cover my face, because when you seemingly are gone, all
that remains in the glance is me, your true face.**

*I am there when - and only when - you are not looking.
I am lost when you search, and found promptly when
you turn your glance away.* **Alas, I am all around you.**
If you only knew, this whole world is a looking glass

and nothing else. All it can be is a reflection of your desires and fears, and yet, I am also there. Can you see me now? Are you willing to pause in looking, so you can see? Just for a moment, relax your intent, put away your thoughts, and tame your judgment. Grace has no face and yet is reflected everywhere. What if I told you, you are the looking glass and I the observer? Did you know that I often see myself reflected in your eyes?

Gently, then, come and sit down by this aging day that is blooming with grace and growing with care. Reflected is you in every glimmer that shines in every corner. The looking glass was the deceiver. All it was, was the wish to see the light of day. And yet it knew it could find it in your glance, in the grace of the kindness of your heart, all in the reflective miracle of your gaze.

∞

Quietly I asked and was quietly answered

A DIALOGUE WITH GOD

❦

Gentle Spirit, I invite your grace upon my heart that I may understand and be consoled. Fear has haunted me for so long, and now that I have resolved my conflicting thoughts, I remain empty, without any doubt, but full of sorrow. What is this emptiness? Where is your luminous presence, and why am I empty of your fullness and not full of your luminous emptiness?

Love answers, not grief, and grace looks not on sorrow. Why then go where all these linger in an antique, forgotten figure resembling an obsolete dance? Now you have remembered, and now you are joyful. Why seek what is not there? All that you thought you had forgotten has been cleansed. Joy remains lonely but cannot feel your sadness, for how could something be what it is not? Are you asking joy to become sorrow? And do you think it possible to imagine grief at the loss of grief? Come empty to be filled. My emptiness is full of your own grace, and my fullness is now and has a new face. Come and stay awhile. Make friends with this newness. God is this changing face, luminous with grace, and incapable of grief and sorrow. It is impossible to think of Him as absent, and this impossibility you ask when you imagine sorrow, when you imagine pain and separation. Ask me of spring, and you will see me. Ask me of pain, and I am lost to you.

Tell me then Spirit of Grace, what is happiness? Why am I not satisfied with the constant unchangeable face of a saint who remains - and remains the same, regardless of weather, regardless of the fury of an ever grieving world?

Have you not asked for all that you have made and all that you have become? Have you not seen all that you have imagined? Have you not changed what is the changeless? My illumined face is yours. Is that not why you call me your father? I call you always, and I know you always. With this call you remember, and like a flower in the spring you open, and again open. And yet you open again without realizing that you never close, for it is impossible to close.

Is that why I have invented the thoughts of duality, dear Spirit? Is that why and how I gave myself a body and a heart? To live awhile and die? To long and to wither away? To desire and to fail?

No, that is not why. In playing you imagined me lost, and closed your eyes. Where is loss if not in an imagined weakness sheltering a lie? And yet in the all possible, daring to dream of the impossible is still godlike. Only a god can imagine a god no more, and yet he is the one imagined so, and he still remains the god imagining. These are childish games, and games are all you seem to be living for. Play awhile, and then come home.

Sorrow and pain and grief are byproducts of a false imagining, of impossibilities, of useless desires that last awhile in a lost world that never was and can never be. And yet a god that imagines so makes it so.

Quietly now, we let all that subside and go to nowhere where it never was. Sorrow is as meaningless as joy is the only reality. Desire is as void as eternity is all fulfilling.

When you closed your eyes, you had no eyes, and what you closed was your heart. When you closed your heart, you gave birth to something that could not last. Your heart has no doors, for the all encompassing cannot be contained. What holds cannot be held. And so, your release becomes meaningless. You are free, and it cannot be otherwise, for it is so. When you closed your eyes, you knew you can still see. Such are the games you play. This knowing is Me, your Father, your Creator, your Sight. That is why when you close your eyes you can see your heart.

Quietly, gently open your eyes again. There is nothing to fear. There is nothing to desire. And there is nothing to need. There is nothing, and that is everything. Quietly know what you always have known. Open your heart for that is your true eye. There is nothing but rejoicing, grace, and peace. Grace cannot be far from the source that created it. Open your heart and see that you are grace. Quietly I call you into the garden. Come and bring a friend. Come to play, for joy awaits you there. Open your heart and see the garden there.

Remember me. Remember spring. The gates to the garden are open beckoning you now. Enter and rejoice. All that was of sorrow and pain, all that, is gone and none of it remains. Nothingness has returned to nothingness, and now only love remains. Come in now. Come in and bring a friend. Come in and play.

❦

Just before the dawn...

A DIALOGUE WITH THE DEVIL

⚜

Waking me up with your frigid breath while it is still dark, what could your business be? This discomfort comes only after vague and confusing dreams of strange visits and unusual messages; all these are uncomfortable calls to an uncommon visitation. Am I being called to a conversation with the shadowy deceiver? Are you feeling left out? Am I not the one who is supposed to initiate these dialogues? You silently stand there beckoning me. Indeed, your calls are strange and your delivery is one of discomfort. Here, I have arrived. What is your message? What is this urge to communicate? And tell me, "dear" shadow, why should I listen?

Am I not usually shy and hidden? Isn't it obvious why my methods remain consistent with my nature? Otherwise you might mistake me for the Holy One and, deceived, you might take pride in my ways and think I was your clever self.

So what have you to tell me? Anything I want to know, or perhaps need to know, to protect myself from your deceiving ways?

My ways might be deceiving. But make no mistake, I cannot deceive but only those who are willing and able to be deceived. My darkness can shy away the eyes that are willingly closed. Isn't this why your movie houses and your most special performing halls darken to the lowest light so you can thoroughly enjoy the illusion on the stage, or the magic of the show? And yes, I admit my light is dim, as it is now in this sweetly shaded dawn. So I have to bring about the darkness, only to be able to dazzle you. Such are stories. All half lies necessarily half lit.

Yes lies, from an old liar. But isn't it better to call me an "actor"? Wouldn't you enjoy my art if you admitted that I might be the maker of illusions, but only at your generous patronage and at your service? Have you ever thought who evil serves? Is it the poor demon that

Just before the dawn...

provides the drama, who at the end is blamed, tied, and banished? Honestly, doesn't that seem a thankless job? Granted, honesty is a rare trait in my business, but yet, even you cannot deny such harsh facts.

The evil ones always serve, as their wickedness is always faithfully present and ready to contrast with the dimly lit lights of dawn. Who can notice your delicate novice dimly lit candlelight but for the wicked dark night? And yet, it is at dawn when I have to offer myself for sacrifice. At dawn, I admit, the dimly lit candle burning through the night triumphs and heralds the first rays of the light, slaying the dragon that everyone loves to see agonized, ridiculed, and banished to the corners of closed closets or under cold rocks. In the shadows I continue to exist, because shamelessly tomorrow I am lured to entertain. Tomorrow, and yet another night.

Tell me in earnest, who is the villain?

Is it not the dark, evil night, ready to die only to glorify? And isn't this why I'm often called the son of dawn or the bringer of light, Lucifer?

Am I supposed to think of you a gentle, harmless demon now? And even perhaps feel sorry for your demise?

Make no mistake, neither you nor I can bear my demise. In show after show the villain must appear to contrast with the light. Isn't it obvious? Isn't it a thankless job?

I admit the shadows come and go. But what merit is there to look in the dark where nothing can be seen? Why should I trust a liar? The one whose purpose is to hide me from myself?

Ah, but how else would you see yourself truly?

Am I supposed to learn the truth from the liar Lucifer?

Humbly I admit truth is not my business. And being a master of lies I have lost all paths to truth. To me truth is yet another lie. What comforts me, although not for long, is my belief in what I make. Admittedly nothing lasts long, and condemned, I have to remake and remake! Lies are fragile things, and evil a delicate trade. Isn't this what your artists are like? Do not answer me. I know that none of my truths stand. What I make must fall. I am the maker of time. I am the entertainer. I am the bringer of pain. But you come willingly to be seduced.

The day has come and I feel naked. The sunlight shame-lessly uncloaks me. I deal only in secrets, and since there are no secrets under the sun, I have to go. I retreat certain of knowing. We shall meet again. Perhaps you will come looking for me. Even if you dwell in light alone, tired of laughter, you will come to the dark halls to be entertained, fooled, and even made to cry. The daylight is here and I have to say farewell, but not goodbye. The shadows always wait; patiently wait for the dimming of light.

And before I go, I give you one gift as I have bestowed on you so many in the past. I have one enemy, and it is not the light. Have you noticed that in every story and in every tale, the only one who can banish me is surrendered and meek? I hate to admit this for I am a master of lies.

The clever one is always my accomplice and the ignorant fool is my demise! Innocence is my foe and not the light, in which you delight!

The dawn has turned to morning and no more of me you will find. But if you look, and carefully so, before the turn of every page, I lurk behind the shadow of every thumb as I deceive and delight, and upon every masterful stage disguised!

❦

A new day…

A DIALOGUE WITH SPRING

Joyful spring, you have arrived with all your glory and sunshine. You are welcome here to my life and to the brave new world breathlessly awaiting you. Tell me what you have brought to share, especially for me?

I greet you gently and bring everything that you had, but refused to see. The joy in my heart is renewal and the wisdom in my breath is forgiveness. The much sought-after love I am well known for, is a lie that fades quickly, as do the flowers and blooms with which I dress all of nature. They wither, they fall, and what remains is the memory of their fragrance reminding you I was here. Beware. I will not stay here long. Do not take me for granted. Do not stay closed, safely tucked in your winter garb. Come out and brave the breeze. The winter is over, and all safety is gone. You cannot, will not, and should not come to me, other than in your luscious empti-

ness and with your raw and beautiful nudity. Come vulnerable. That is the only way I will accept you, and only when I accept you, can you accept me. Spring is not for the fainthearted. No. Spring is not for the weak. Spring is strength. You were blind and could not see that true strength is really in the frail, vulnerable, delicate blossom that flutters in the wind. It seems to live for a moment in the brilliant sunlight, doomed to be torn by the passionate storm. Fall it may, and a memory it will be, but now, only now, it lives in eternity. Spring is now. Do you see? Now it lives forever. This is the gift of spring. Do you dare to see?

I am not sure if I like you much, capricious spring, especially if you do not plan to stay long, and ruthlessly threaten to leave.

Spring is new love. How could it stay if it is to remain new? For strangely so, it has to go to be true to its newness. In order to remain eternally new it has to escape the prison of your permanence. For what faith brings, joy destroys, just as what love reveals, security shamelessly hides. Spring is all about madness. I am the revealer

A new day...

of all that was securely hidden under the blankets of an aging winter. Spring has come, and all that is no more.

It is true, spring comes and quickly goes. Spring is holy, spring is divine. This is what whoever lives in spring truly knows. That moment you call Now is the place where spring eternally grows. There is no secret that spring holds, for spring is an opening. So come to the feast you call this season. Here I reveal to you your lie! Spring is no season! Spring is your perpetual you.

☙❧

Upon the undeliverable promise…

A DIALOGUE WITH LUST

❧

I find myself waiting for you disinterestedly thumb-ing through books and looking at the magnifi-cent grandeur of the vernal awakening that, like a naked babe, runs in the chill of the early hours of a promising day. I feel nothing but a nagging need waiting for you, your promise to come. And, still waiting, I am disconnected, foreign to my own space and air. When it comes, it will be. It is not here yet, but when it comes, it promises to bring with it the spring. But now, I am not interested. Nothing really matters. It is not here yet.

Waiting I am seduced, I am engaged in all that I do not want, the lies, the deceptions, the betrayals; all this because I do not care.

Spring comes with heavy clouds that rain and pour all day. I am blind, I cannot see, I am waiting.

Is it you that ravages me, or is it your promise to take me away? Why do I so freely submit to your lies? Why do I want you so badly when I know quite well that, by all accounts and letters, you are bad?

It is me and not my promise that betrays you over and over. All this is because you cannot, or better said, you are not willing, to see me as I am now, here and with you as I always have been. My promise never comes, but I have been with you forever. I am the oldest lie, the deepest secret you have kept hidden from yourself. Yet you're coming back to me again and again. Every promise given is an invitation to descend deeper on the staircase of deception and pain. If you unveil me, taking away the luscious covering of velvet and silk, you can gently look and see me. I am lust, your oldest friend and enemy. Gently look, only gently, for I cannot bear harsh and honest glares.

I live in a half light darkened by a heavy heart, burdened by falsely perfumed breaths and the powdered imperfections of an old professional. Come closer and I'll give you what you are here for. I give you my promise; no, not to fulfill, but to keep you hungry, although we both know you are indeed full.

Why do you do that? Why such evil? Why such heartache? Are you the devil?

No, I am not the devil, for in me there is not even a trace of evil. Actually, in me there is no trace of anything. I am the emptiness that never fails to entrap the willing fool. I am gentle, kind, calm. I am a calling to a passion that you have forgotten you are. And yet you are willing to sacrifice all of who you are for my promise. Look at me clearly, and you will see me.

I am really an angel. Don't you consider angels kind, soft, and dreamy? Airy so they can fly? And don't you fancy the flight of a passion entangled in naked arms and thighs? Never mind the wings. Never mind that angels fly away. Isn't temperance fair? It needs to be light in its flight, necessarily temporary. For if not for distance, what use is of calling? What use of a distant song? What use of a golden voice, never mind that it nags and cries? Pay attention to its resonance. What you call beauty is its allure. Have you forgotten what it felt to be in the arms of an angel?

Come now, come. You must pay first. And make sure you pay gladly, for all you're paying ensures your fulfillment. When you pay you know you deserve. I promise you now, as I always have. Only if you wait, as they say, good will come. And do not call it bad, for if you do you will be even more deceptive than me. Call it good, and then you will see that my promises are fulfilled, with nothing less than more promises. Especially for you.

Come upon my arms to rest...

A DIALOGUE WITH DEATH

❧

Hesitantly I approach you. But make no mistake, I have no such intentions to cross mysterious rivers or step on such downward journeys as did the unfortunate Orpheus. No, make no such mistake. I approach you only to inquire and understand. Why do you bear such a dark heart and deep sorrow? How can you bear your own gross weight and not collapse into oblivion and an eternal black fate?

Why are you the end to everything? Why have you forgotten, or perhaps never knew what you so callously rob others of? I wonder if I can bear to have such a conversation. For how could my voice enter an endless cave and reach an unreachable end? Who is there to listen? Who is peering at me in the dark? Or is it all my imagination?

I am here just as you imagine me, ugly or grave, dark and somber, or morbid and grim. Just the way you require me to be, so I am. Just so. I am not here to claim you. All truth be said, it is you that often claim me. I am your slave, ready to serve you, as you wish.

Serve, you say? What use of death? Are you a pause, or an end? And what of your cruel intrusions and ruthless interruptions? Are you not the bringer of sorrows and unkind separations?

No, I am not unkind, for kindness rests on understanding, and you arrive always gently into my arms, understanding only when you arrive. Rest from unkind toil is not sorrow. Escape from torment is not separation, but reunion. I am the bringer of peace.

Is it not you who kill? Is it not you who wage wars? And is it not you who separate in the name of your virtues, laws, and gods? And in doing so, I am slavishly employed by the same hypocrisy that condemns and abolishes me. Truth be told, don't you need rest from your childish games? Don't you require a pause after each glare? A refreshing blink and tear after each judgment and unfair assessment? Is it not hypocrisy to call a restful night the abyss, and the bringer of comfort the reaper grim?

With every blink of an eye you call on me, and every night we embrace and practice lying side by side. How unjust to call your dutiful servant a foe, and how unkind to look at the cleanser of sorrows with fear and contempt. Am I not called by you when you have decimated what you had built, employed only to recycle? And if truly all there is is a cycle, isn't "end" a lie? What can end that is created eternal?

I am death, the dark side, yet only dark because of your refusal to see. Dark is the grave, my workshop. But make no mistake, my work is alchemy. What you give me I remake, and so what you call "this life", perpetuates. Your corpses, useless after your use, I reuse to make flowers. On the same pastures in which you have buried your grieving wars I paint a scenery of love, where gentle grass and flowers grow, where you can come and go. Mysterious you call me. True, but isn't that because you have hidden me so grossly? What you come to fear at the end, and yet the end is not so. Isn't it madness to fear rest? And isn't it unkind to make the night a sleepless nightmare?

Do not seek to abolish me. Abolish your unkindnesses instead. And as long as you insist on wars and killings, and dark imaginings that scare you, call on me to repair your soul.

So be kind to this servant who willingly serves, for there is only ignorance to beware. Death comes, and there is life again. What seems an exit is an entrance, a circle really. You should not care.

Upon a full day's work…

A DIALOGUE WITH THE BODY

Tired and worn out, you call upon me, dear faithful companion and fellow traveler. I notice you as you kindly remind me of the long day, the length measured with every notion and invitation to comfort you with my aware attention. I was beside you and yet beside myself about you. My destination more precious than the journey, I mindlessly neglected my precious companion.

Dear friend, handsome and strong, neutral and kind, at the end of this long journey, you were my destiny. And yet, I sought the illusions and shadows of the dream of arrival, when all I did was close my sight to you in hopes to see myself projected where I was not, being what I am not, attempting to become better when I was already the best. Will you forgive me? Can we sit at rest again and enjoy our company in stillness? Can you forgive my transgressions, ignorant demands, and hollow desires?

Gently now, let's pause as you arrive to realize the happy marriage of the chariot and the charioteer. I am at your service, pliable, plausible, and patient. I apply your demands to what you built me to be. I withstand and outstand the strain of the storms you desire and the shadows you crawl into. We both travel, and when you require courage I let you hide in me. When you require adventure I am there to thrill. And yet, I have to remain your servant, obedient and present. But make no mistake, I am never a slave.

Although I am the straps that bind you, my limitations are designed to teach you your limitless potentials. As I become the boundaries of your domain, I also become the hearth that houses the fire of your love. Gently I hold you so you can feel the flutter of your wings and still remember that you can fly far and unfettered. When you are too burdened by the weight of judgments hiding in the shadowy landscape of your nightmares, we lie together in stillness as I let you recover and rest.

I am never tired. It is you who demands the explanation and invents the weakness that you lay upon me to which I am obedient. I take you where you want to go even if that destination serves not our purpose. Yet, when we arrive, I make you the innocent as I take all the blame, costing me my shape and form, as I'm echoed in your awareness as pain and strain.

And when you desire playful love and joining with another, although you break away and fly, forgetting your fidelity to me, I come along to meet the servant of another master. I try to serve two masters knowing well that I am bound to fail. Pretense in joining of the already joined, ridiculous as it seems, I make a dance of it, to please a friend and fight a foe, and yet it is not so. I will strike or kiss a friend or foe, although truly the difference I don't know. What I know is how to shelter and hold you as a good companion can, but also I do advise you in all that comes to pass. Through me you see and smell, you taste and touch, and to yourself and others you seem to tell invented tales, a calculus that builds the road we travel. You make of me the storyteller to tell your story every time. And so, to time you bind me, leading me from birth to death, and to all that seem achievement but in truth are passing dreams. And when you are done, as we know I serve you well, you lay me down at the end of the journey of a long day.

Upon the sweat of the brow...

A DIALOGUE WITH WORK

⚜

They asked me for a favor and I answered out of obligation. Now my reward is two aching hands. This working day, meekly submitting to the daily grind, I deplore you, for you have found me condemned to toil and to be a slave of time. Unfortunate as it may seem, you, work, my work, to which I hopelessly attend, robs me of my vigor and youth. And at the end, when you have exhausted me of all my resources, you crown me with the passing glory of the wreath of accomplishment. You claim I am the builder. What a hollow claim from you, the destroyer of dreams.

Why are you so cruel? Why do you make suffering out of labor, and in your simplicity of purpose all my days you take? To what end you dare to end me, leaving me worn and old after each day, my only reward the salty dew upon a frowning face? And resigned alas, I find myself the following morning at your door again, knocking to enter, and not long after, sorry to remain.

Silent I remain. I am your work, the only thing you can really claim, and the only thing in which, in truth, remains yours. No one knows his lot. I am the assigner of destinies. Although I may seem the thief of youth who claims your labor, I profess it is you who makes your life a profession.

My kind attendant and diligent friend, I was meant to be your mistress and a playmate. But there entered your serious judge and hooded defender, and you made an executioner of me. My call was only a joyful song and an invitation to play, but sadly so only a calling you made of me. What was meant to be a sparrow's playful dance and feathered spring song to joy, you made a harsh whistle and a calling to toil. You, it is you who made and make. And yet, I still remain a sweet bird's song, a joyful dance, and an invitation to play.

What you build is of no consequence. All that you offer, a waste. Your helping hand, a passing notion. Your courage to save others, nothing but a shadow puppet saga. *Your worries, your frowning face, your burdened heart are slaves. Your feeding frenzy upon your time, this ignorant treatment of all things and people you claim as fellow travelers toward the same aim, is hiding your true enemy. He is your true employer of toil and the one to whom you freely give your time and strength. Greed is the never satisfying monster that has made a whip out of my feathers and a sting out of my kissing lips. How unkind to treat your brushes without respect, for their soft, sensual dance allows the divine movement of your hand to make and bless the canvas. And what we make is just the reflection of your smile. What have you lost when you forgot to laugh? Upon your salty frown, what can the brush record? Now that the dance has become a total discord?*

Stop, I say. Stop all this mockery of what you made of me and you. Pause a moment from your frenzied commotion and mad rush to make. That is not what your creator meant when so grandly He made you.

You were meant to dance and not merely walk, so it is wise to see that every time you walk, you dance. Your speech a sweet song, so stop and listen, for every time you talk, you sing. And what, you ask, is your song like? Truly I tell you, although to sweetness you seem temporarily blind, the music from your limbs and tongue, turn the wheels of a universe. A heaven full of angels sings your song, even from your silent dreams. And in your graceful body movement, all celestial bodies dance to a harmony you cannot yet hear and to a melody you have long forgotten.

So remember now when your seeming hand movements build buildings, that which you see, that which you think greater than you, is not so. It cannot be. What in reality you made is a grand symphony, a music, that till eternity sounds, will touch all there is and all that will be. And that touch, that movement is the reflection of your heart, your core, and what your creator made. And made He you as Himself, for love can only love make. As He made you by His love, in reality you also make everything by love. How mistaken you have been to see your love as labor, for labor and love are not the same.

Upon the sweat of the brow...

So rest awhile and look again. Your hands are no hands that give pain. And when you smile no salty frown remains. Your work is love and nothing else. So rest awhile and begin again. And knowing so let your lips only say kisses, and your limbs only sing music, and know your work only as play.

.

Upon the breaking of the bread...

A DIALOGUE WITH FOOD

☙❧

You call me to the kitchen and I come expectant, knowing I will find you. You are here preparing to love me. I know for I have been here before, and I long to come back, especially when you call me. I find myself drunk and seduced by the aroma of love, of what I know will fulfill me and transform me just as the alchemist transforms base metal to gold.

I have learned to remember my creator in your presence, and I have learned that to share you is to extend my essence and my love. Tell me then, nourishing food, how am I different from you? Am I not just a pawn in the game of consumption? Are you not what feeds me only to prepare me to feed another? Am I not just a means to fatten for a feast of other worms and beast? And tell me then, why in grief I am to abstain and hunger recalling a famine and fast? Why at weddings, upon a celebration, you are the center; yet when I indulge and crave you, you seem distant and can never satisfy? What magic is food, and what food is magic that fools me again and again? Food, speak to me, not in your usual ways as sirens do, seduced to consume you as you in reality consume me.

Feast or famine, all are false. Both are extremes that cause your hunger. Don't be fooled. That hunger is not for me. Hunger never calls you, but imposes like an unwanted guest. Craving is a fooling friend, and nothing but a villain in sheep's clothing. Not I. Not there you will find me. But if you simply look, I was what greeted you first when you arrived shortly after leaving her womb. When you expectedly sucked upon the nipple of her love, I nourished you, rushing to comfort, competing only with the gentle loving embrace you felt in her arms. I was the milk her breast gave, and so and always I remain.

It is you who makes other things of me. Upon your magical creations, pretending to nourish your faith, you miss my simple gifts. You spice my simple comfort and make a feast of a simple fate. I am always here to nourish, and nothing else. When you add, and make new creations, that feast, that art, that concoction, amazing as it seems, feeds a need that I cannot heed. Simple food is simple only when simply seen. In its simplicity it nourishes and satisfies, not a need, but a function.

The cycle of nourishment is a beautiful basket woven tightly with joy. As other living life shares its grace with you, it is only because you are part of its own fabric. All of it is food. All of it that you call a feast is a joyful sharing, and does not ebb and flow. In giving of itself it becomes more. For in its consuming it becomes its consumer, and when consumed it becomes the whole. The mother's milk that fed you once, in you will also feed, for as she lovingly nourished you, you also learned lovingly to nourish so. When you come to me, whether be it at high noon or upon the breaking of the bread at suppertime, see your nourishment as an extended love that becomes you, and through extension, the unbroken thread that holds the whole.

Do not add. For as you do, you obscure your understanding, your comfort, and your wisdom. What you call a spice is only a medicine to cure an unwilling heart. And what you cherish as a delight is only a false promise to an already starving child. Food is love only when it is simply seen and simply loved. Mother's milk, that's what I am, and that's all I can be. Add a spice and a dash of salt, and all that magic you exalt might delight a king's palate and create a feastly taste, but it will not necessarily make it nourishment.

Find me in the laughter of a song heard in the dream of a babe, safely in slumber in the arms of its mother. There I am, doing what I do best, gently nourishing you, preparing, repairing, and caring for what will wake up with a gentle thirst and a desire for more. I am always giving and always there, like an unbroken and unbreakable promise to nurture you now, as you learn to care for others.

⁕

Upon gentle hands…

A DIALOGUE WITH LOVE

✦

I learned of you first when I felt your gentle touch, and then I knew of love. Although I have read in books about heroic measures and sacrifices beyond comprehension, all that lovers do, only to get a chance to embrace. Only to garner their faith and glimpse each other's grace. Tell me, love, whoever you are, is it true that you are grand but, are you also humble and gentle like a summer kiss upon a fair maid?

Are you grand and small, gentle and tall, yet also dark and seductive? Or are you heroic and swift? Which is it? Love, tell me truthfully, are you for real? I still recall your gentle hands, that gentle embrace which upon my innocent flesh felt like holiness.

Ay, love, seemingly a faded flower on a summer day, gentle yet certain, I am a concoction, sure and certain, constant in my faith, and assuring to the moth that dares the flame. Like a doorway, all inviting into a garden, cool and fresh, set for you to come and rest after a seemingly long journey on a dusty path to nowhere.

Gentle, yes, but not embracing. I am an invitation, gentle and kind, never a call or a command, neither swift nor heroically rushing, always sure and certain of my fate, knowing myself and the final destination of all saints and sinners alike. Now, as your love, I dare to ask: Do you miss me? Are you lonely and afraid? Do you think of me as gone and faded? Am I a wish that only lives in dreams of sorrow, destined for great tragedies and unfulfillable fates of folly? Am I forced to wear costumes soiled by bloody daggers hopelessly piercing hearts that are not brave enough to bear me though heroic enough to submit to death? Who is the hero that cannot bear the pain? And where is the pain, but in a heart full of revenge darkened by hopeless dares?

I do remain gentle and soft, like a gentle blanket with dreams I subdue all nightmares and wait for all tales to tame. What you call love, not an imitation, not even a *glimpse or a resemblance of me it contains. What you call love is more an adventure into the wild with heroes who battle unfairness and dragons, and with knights who fight their fate with anger and might. And still, love calmly and gently remains a rose.*

Patiently I wait certain of your fate. When the children's imaginary dragons are slain in their swords fight, the boy and girl alike will grow to see the rose that was always there and still remains. The boy and girl, only in childish games are different, distinguished by their garb and manner, insisting on playing different roles. But upon the gentle hands of their embrace they become one, the patiently waiting grace, the rose. And so with grace, forgiveness dawns to brighten their darkest nightmares and their night of sorrows. Upon the sun shining from their hearts, united by grace, all is lost between them, and only their true essence, love, remains.

And so what died in this union was neither lover nor mate. That is not what unites the two, but rather a certain fate that all must return to, the heart that has created them as one.

The hands that touched you, were the gentle messengers, like the wings of an angel that showed you the way. There is no night that can hide, no clutter that can obscure the way to your own heart today. As you recall those hands that cared, your hands thus become the hands that strip your divisions away. And as you have been touched, so will you show another pair of gentle hands how they, too, are wings on a beloved angel.

✕

Upon a burdened heart...

A DIALOGUE WITH GRIEF

⚜

Joy seems far away. Love has lost its way, and now all my days and nights seem gray and dull. Here, is a burdened heart like a heavy cloud that is here to stay. What are you here to claim? Is the grief of a lost day, a chance to glance at a face forgotten, long and somber? Tell me, grief, what business is this coming around on a hot summer day claiming joy and turning day into night? Heaviness burdens shoulders, and now what carried a love carries only broken promises.

You have taken the day away, and staring me in the face, grief, you seem to be the thief of life. Surrendered to your numbing claws I give my burdened heart to your unforgiving eyes as mine are dampened by tears, and clouded by the sorrow of a thousand years. What business have you here?

I am the dumb and deaf child of a grieving father who has forgotten all his children. I wander aimlessly from door to door, asking now for what I cannot have and wishing for all that is not there. I cannot say, and I do not understand. Saying and understanding brought me here. But I live in a different dream where my business is being, not doing or saying. I hear no joy, and I see no light.

I do not cry, but I am silent. I do not grieve, but I witness calmly that which is unwelcome, and all that is bitter and charred. Nothing escapes me in my circle of grief, where I go round and round inviting a stare, peeling away the weathered and burned covers of young and old hearts that dared to love, dared to care, and now in loss and sadness, aimlessly surrender to me.

I strip away all the heart's desires. I strip away all hopes and dreams. But what seems cruel and savage, this peeling away, is really a renewal, returning the dead to the dying, so that the living can stay to become unburdened in the depth of unbearable burdens where no shell can remain. What can you do but surrender to a truth that a thousand lies a single lie can bear? But a thousand truths are not enough to gladden a heart caught in my snare.

Come to me you must, for there is no other way to let the temporal perish, and to free your true nature. How else would you leave behind what burdens your flight into the awareness of light but with the sadness of lead, heavier than you can bear? Your wings and feathers you understand, and in this understanding you become whole and unbroken. What seemed to have dipped you into the depth of darkness removes your heavy heart of despair and bares your soul to an emptiness that holds your heart of joy.

This joy takes flight when you return from letting go, and only when doing so, in grief, in my sacred circle, you are cleansed and purified. The destiny of the broken is to heal, and the fate of the forgotten is to remember. And so, the child returns to the Father who understands. And now the child can know the Father who can never forget. Sorrow has no place among the living, and while you forget life, my heaviness darkens your burdened mind.

I break the hardened shell of your seemingly separated heart, while tears wash you clean of sorrows, purifying and reuniting you with the heart of hearts. Turn your glance away. Let the dead bury the dead in my midst as you freely fly to your freedom.

Lost in the joy of our visit…

A DIALOGUE WITH FRIENDSHIP

꧁꧂

Finding you by my side again, my beloved friend of ages, and in this moment, in the glimmer of your eye, I am lost. Free of time, free of places and occasions you bring me to the joy of eternity, to the silence of the loudest laughter hidden in our miraculous smile. We look at each other and we lose ourselves, erasing all moments we were apart as the music of our lives, continues uninterrupted by everything else. Our togetherness is the basket that contains the fruits of our joy. We dissolve, becoming whole again, as we forget we ever were a broken string, now mended by the master weaver's hand.

Our friendship is a multicolored tapestry woven tightly. We take it lightly, using it often to shelter our shoulders from a cold draft, or step on it to dry our feet on rainy days. Yet now that I look, I see you, dear friendship, precious and loyal. And when

I see you, all else disappears and only you remain, patiently, gently, silently, carefully, wisely. Are you the safe keeper of the gods? Are you the treasurer of all loving deeds and thoughts? Friendship, tell me, are you what the sages call the most sacred of all?

Burden me not, for no task is a burden to a willing heart. When you come to my garden, and with vows you join with another's heart, you help me weave the universe of love with yet another gentle knot. All that there is sits in this banquet of love, set on and supported by a beautiful blanket of joy, woven as a gentle yet strong tapestry made by countless knots. The master weaver Himself prepared it so, for every time two lives have crossed and joined in the joy of friendship, a knot has marked that sacred love.

As grand as all the universe might seem, none of it sits disconnected and alone. Everything there is lies on this blanket that sweetly holds all there was, is, and to become. And so, nothing is a greater gift exchanged than a loving friendship, not unlike an often traveled path be-

tween two neighboring hearts. What is the whole world for but to serve my holy purpose? And what worthy cause or endeavor is accomplished but by the love of coupled souls walking under the arc of friendship? Neither the greatest lovers nor the closest kin can compare to the blessing of oneness that a true friendship brings, for the rings of friendship are sacred so that no limit, earthly or not, can confine and break its silent vows.

Gently then, upon the face of your companions behold the miracle of what I am. Such a friendship is your greatest gift. For by allowing me to live within your hearts, this miraculous love, unequal yet grander than all the universal laws, is projected onto stars, eternally shining with an inextinguishable light. This eternal light, reflected in the glimmer of your eyes, when all the temporal is lost in the joy of your joining one another, this eternal fire, burns all barriers keeping you apart.

This union is love, and in such joining all else dissolves. And you, eternal and pure love, unlimited and always, as you were created and remain forever, are realized.

From the glimmer in your eyes to the distant stars at night is but a short journey from recognition to embrace. So remember to keep me near and dear to your breast. As you journey west, from sunrise to sunset, I guide you safely home to the stars.

⚜

Broken at your doorsteps...

A DIALOGUE WITH SURRENDER

❧

Having arrived tired and broken at your doorstep, nothing is left of my long line of defense. Here I offer all of me, which seemingly I value little. Broken and humbled, I am resigned to a fate unknowable to my cluttered mind and exhausted limbs.

I cannot wage war any longer. All that there is has claimed victory over me, and life has swallowed me whole condemning me to the fate of Jonah. To the dark of the jaws of death I have been submitted. Now in the belly of life I am confined to be what it wishes.

In this darkness of unknown and unimagined I feel the warmth and integration of a liberated mind unburdened by the responsibility of judgment and command. I am yours, and all that was mine, however small and insignificant, is also offered you completely. I am surrendered to the life of surrender, to you, the great integrator.

Why are you so hungry to devour all that strays and demands individuality? At the end of all vain paths and winding passions you stand waiting and accepting. Are you the grand consolidator of everything? Are you the real death, the great motionless mover and destroyer of all unruly dreams?

Quietly I come to you and quietly I offer you strength, wisdom, and the knowing of all that there is. But alas, quiet joys are often dismissed as idle, and great strength as unreal by struggling dreams of fancy and fate-less furies of battle. Quietly I wait, and patiently I embrace wrecks and wretches who abandon worthless struggles. What is defeat, but a weak idea ill-conceived and mal-intentioned? What is war, but self hatred?

Quietly and patiently all that is deserved is received, and all that is bestowed is assimilated. I am the fabric of all events, and the bringer of all gifts. Only the blind and temporarily insane ignore the very ground they walk on as they imagine fights of folly. Upon awakening to the reality of their cause, they come to bless the security of my grounding grip and sheltering safety.

What is, is yours. Denying it only blinds you and injures your dream by turning the glory of your days into nightmares. Upon such disasters I apply my quiet understanding, embracing you and sheltering your broken wings and weary dreams.

But make no mistake. I am not home only to broken guests, but also to the brave and wise who submit their faith before the forces of their fate collapse. They restrain their delusions knowing well that the art of the inevitable far exceeds their small imagined tempests and struggles. As they submit their fate to me they also become the fabric that grounds the inevitable, thus joining in the universal chorus of life. This greatness is lost to everyone who aimlessly battles for bounty and misses the true strength that is everyone's inheritance. When all storms have passed, when all hearts are calmed, albeit seemingly by defeat, everyone comes home to my banquet, and friend and foe find brotherhood at last.

So come early and come often, for I safely keep your strength and your nobility. All battles are in vain, all struggles pointless, for all who battle and struggle must come to me. All must come, for there is nowhere else to go as long as coming and going you fancy. And as your hand submits itself to the writer and your song to the singing voice, I give strength to all your actions, and glory and purpose to your joy.

∞

Upon the brow of the prophet...

A DIALOGUE WITH FAITH

⚜

Knowing you has delivered me from many a storm. Understanding the miracles of your handiwork, I have relied on you when all else seemed lost, and despair remained my only alternative. Faithful faith, loyal to all seasons and constant as a rock, what is your secret? What and how do you deliver this magic, that makes heroes out of fools, and knights out of petty warriors?

You must know all the intricacies and laws whereby destinies unfold. Is it true that you are both what every fate is made of, and the only means by which one can escape his snare? Faith in what, I am told, does not matter, for in you alone all is lost or all is saved. Tell me, enigmatic friend, how are all your workings set? Why and how does all this power through you prevail?

Faith to the faithless is a toy, and often the victim of possession. I am often made a ploy to bewilder the unknowing, poor, and joyless. Have you noticed as I arrive in lives that had lost me for a while, I become a passion and obsession; yet to the quiet and grateful, I convey a knowing that no church or temple can endorse and no grand master or teacher can promote? This knowing is my gift to you with which you can move mountain on the wings of a desire to love with an unchanging heart and unfettered vision. Fates are written faithfully upon the brow of every traveler. But he becomes the prophet who chooses his fate with faith.

Look upon all your brothers, and it will not be hard to see who among them walk unfettered by whims and doubts that toss and turn the masses. Yet to the ones who choose my path, all others become the saints and prophets. Careful, then, upon your calling to this faithful friend to come, for as I come to you I bring a strength and vision no less than a martyr's path. What you give up is all your reins that masquerade as your strength. Upon giving me your will, you learn that a whole universe you build. Understanding such a task can shake dominions and heavens. The creator's strength and grace lie in such surrender, so that a whole Eden can be made from a mustard seed.

I would caution you in deed and thought - in all you set forth in me - be it serpents tempting your fall from grace, or endless joyful gardens housing you safely, or even glorious reunions in one holy place. That which you entrust to me, that I make your fateful fate. Knowing such a gift, no record or book of names can hinder you. So choose and choose me discerningly, for that you give me not I shall take, be it doubt, debt, or doomsday fate. And so I am the greatest of all gifts. In me all can rise and fall, and thus I can become the guiding light that shines your pathway home. For without such light, every heart strays, lost in desolation, far from the joyous purpose of reunion, and remains in a darkened place. Within the safety of my dominion, the certainty of every step is assured. And the light that warms your heart shines beyond its boundaries, lighting the way for those you lovingly keep close. With this light, a single purpose

I do make, joining every shining ray, turning every doubting darkness into a clear and brilliant day. Thus, the shining vision of the prophet, destined to light your way, transforms your every step to joy and turns your path to a highway.

✖

On the light wings of joy...

AND A DIALOGUE WITH HOPE

꙳

With true conviction I search and find you. Wherever I look, you are there. In every corner and in every dark place, I see an eternal flame, albeit sometimes a faint glimmer, a persistent candle: Where I look, I find you.

Seemingly a miraculous existence, untouched by all doubts and dares, you burn, lighting and guiding the steps of the seekers of joy. But joy is not your makeup, and passion is not your flare. Are you wisdom affecting all outcomes, a knowing that bridges to the future, making a stepping stone of every error and failed attempt?

How do you do that? Amazed at your powers, I ask: Are you my greatest ally in this realm and in all others? I seem to accomplish anything while you light and guide my way. Hope, are you my crowning glory, and the star of my night and day?

Indeed the burning candle at the window guides the way even in the darkest nights, when the moon and stars are lost behind thick clouds of distrust, and doubt rules your night and day. I am that knowing that lives in the human heart, untouchable by all logical and illogical proof that seeks to extinguish my eternal flame.

This flame was set by your Creator upon the joyous wings that gave flight to His imagination, creating you and Him the same. I am thus bright and eternal, illuminating all you know and see upon the bridge; inventing knowledge and a million worlds anew.

There is nothing that can hinder or obscure your view as I help you see my purpose in the grandeur of your arrival. Your little candle illuminates a whole universe. In this light of joy, sorrow, its path, and memory are all forgot. The bridge, your guiding candle, and even I disappear. And rightly so; a sun and shining star, the true reality that you are - that, and only that, remains.

Then I will hear you say you traveled light upon my wings of joy. As you dreamed of joy, a life of joy you lived and made. "All is well at last!" you will say, as wellness you imagine. For what is hope but a desire that fathers all fates and faith? In this beginning, we will end, knowing well that wellness was always in the plan. For He who planned us so, indeed planned well.

Thus remember that your hope always justified the grandest growth, like the seeds grow to become the mighty arbor amidst a spacious heart. So upon my light wings lightly rest, and know your journey is of Joy.

Epilogue

Now the view from the windows of the house has changed. Stillness has nested in my space, and although September teases the garden with an occasional chilled night, fast moving high clouds threaten to pour but never do. Looking out I see a sleepy cheerful view, tired of playing in the summer sun and ready for a change. Everything seems to be waiting: waiting for the cooler air and autumn to arrive. Everything is waiting, except me.

I have arrived. It has been a long journey into the night where I have met many monsters and gods. I have to admit, I am satisfied. I heard clearly and understood. I traded my heavy heart for a lighter mind. It seems the day has dawned again rendering my path visible. I am neither alone nor feel lonely, but I am grateful for the wise murmur of the now silent voices. I have heard all I needed to hear, and now I am ready to begin.

What I expected never came. The promise of the new day gradually turned into the certainty of release. With each dialogue I witnessed part of me awake, speak, and leave. Fear of loss, lurking beneath my longing, reared its ugly face, stared at me, and left. The thousand faced demon that I had long nurtured spoke with different voices and transformed as it assumed different aspects. With every inquiry and supplication it reached far into the wilderness of my soul. And so we dialogued.

Each dialogue brought back myself to me. A self I had known but conveniently forgotten. In searching for what I thought was rightly mine, I remembered to whom I rightfully belonged. My longing, now renewed with a bittersweet resolve, turned my sweet tears bitter with the avarice of salt and blinded every vain desire with an inner light of halt. Now I wanted nothing, as I understood nothing and refused what I had become.

Relentlessly abandoning belief, I traversed my winding maze of mind. From a waiting self to a lying vision and from a false promise to a neglected need, this transfigured voice gently carried my craven greed. Fallen, helpless, and confessing my need, I witnessed this voice become an angel beyond my wildest dreams, who brought me back from where I had not been to where I could not have dreamed.

Now safely here and forever home, I remain beloved in His thought. And with a blooming spring in my heart, joyfully to Joy I return.

And so, blessings to the all blessed and to the awakened, amen.

༄

Acknowledgments

⚜

I owe much gratitude to everyone who advised me on how to edit this work. It was a privilege to write it and an even greater blessing to have had a band of angels encouraging and guiding its editing process. I am certain that almost all my scribal errors were found and banished by the wonderful editors that so generously volunteered their efforts and time.

I am truly indebted to Ms. Judith Judson who lovingly guided me in understanding how and what I wrote. Her knowledge and love of the English language was truly inspiring. My loving gratitude to my friend Nancee Camuti who listened to every chapter and convinced me not to abandon what I had written and also to the kindness of my gentle friend Michael Shawn Wright. I am also indebted greatly to my yoga teacher and beloved friend Corry Rooks for her understanding, recognizing, and guiding my first steps towards editing this work. Her editorial remarks undoubtedly improved this work in numerous ways as her guidance continues to improve my posture and maintain my physical health.

Many friends and family contributed with editorial and encouraging comments, too many to mention here. However, the most beloved force that bridged decades of distance and found me needing her loving guidance was my High School English Teacher Miss Helen (Eleni Hidiroglou) who continues to teach me the beauty and miraculous force of the English language. She is truly the best English teacher in the world.

Acknowledgments

My heart is full with the love for all my life companions, from Julian, whom this work is lovingly dedicated, to my two great earthly angel sisters Meroulla and Zizella who have been watching over me from the moment I was born. Also, I extend my infinite gratitude to my beloved teacher and friend Marshall Ball and his family who continue to be a guiding light in my life.

I must apologize for not mentioning everyone who continues to inspire and sustain me and ask for your forgiveness for not mentioning you by name. If you have ever met me in person or otherwise, I wish you to know that my life and life's work, all of it, is truly dedicated to you and your happiness.

"To heal is to make happy." I was healed in many ways in the process of writing and editing this work, hence I am forever grateful to the gentle kind source that so generously entrusted me with bringing these words to the world.

www.ingramcontent.com/pod-product-compliance
Lightning Source LLC
Chambersburg PA
CBHW021338090426
42742CB00008B/652